D0792216

## Outlaws and Lawmen of the Wild West

# BUTCH CASSIDY

## Carl R. Green
### ✦ and ✦
## William R. Sanford

ENSLOW PUBLISHERS, INC.

44 Fadem Road         P.O. Box 38
Box 699              Aldershot
Springfield, N.J. 07081    Hants GU12 6BP
U.S.A.                   U.K.

**Library of Congress Cataloging-in-Publication Data**

Green, Carl R.
    Butch Cassidy / Carl R. Green and William R. Sanford.
        p. cm. — (Outlaws and lawmen of the wild west)
    Includes bibliographical references and index.
    ISBN 0-89490-587-2
        1. Cassidy, Butch, b. 1866—Juvenile literature. 2. Outlaws—West
(U.S.)—Biography—Juvenile literature. 3. West (U.S.)—
History—1860-1890—Juvenile literature. 4. West (U.S.)—
History—1890-1945—Juvenile literature. [1. Cassidy, Butch, b.
1866. 2. Robbers and outlaws.] I. Sanford, William R. (William
Reynolds), 1927- . II. Title. III. Series: Green, Carl R.
Outlaws and lawmen of the wild west.
F595.C362G74 1995
364.1′55′092—dc20
[B]                                                         94-24844
                                                               CIP
                                                                AC

Printed in the United States of America

10 9 8 7 6 5 4 3 2 1

**Illustration Credits:** John E. Allen, Inc., p. 41; Colorado Historical Society,
p. 16; Denver Public Library, Western History Department, pp. 9, 23, 27;
Carl R. Green and William R. Sanford, p. 11; Image 15-3, Union Pacific
Museum Collection, p. 24; Image 15-6, Union Pacific Museum Collection,
p. 28; Image 15-7, Union Pacific Museum Collection, p. 31; Utah State
Historical Society, pp. 14, 35, 37; Wyoming State Museum, pp. 20, 21.

**Cover Illustration:** Michael David Biegel

# CONTENTS

# AUTHORS' NOTE

This book tells the true story of an outlaw known as Butch Cassidy. Butch and his gang, the Wild Bunch, were as well known a hundred years ago as rock stars are now known. Their exploits appeared in newspapers, magazines, and dime novels. In more recent years Butch has been featured in movies and on television. Some of the stories have been made up, but many are true. To the best of the authors' knowledge, all of the events described in this book really happened.

# 1

# A SHOOTOUT IN BOLIVIA

Sometime around 1901 the daring western outlaw Butch Cassidy dropped out of sight. Americans were left to wonder about his fate. Almost thirty years later the *Washington Post* printed what seemed to be a final answer. "BUTCH IS DEAD" a headline shouted.[1]

The news story was based on a 1930 magazine article. Arthur Chapman, writing in *Elks Magazine*, retold the story of Cassidy's life.[2] Butch, Chapman wrote, had been a western Robin Hood. Butch and his gang, he told his readers, stole from rich cattle barons, bankers, and railroad tycoons. After each job they vanished into a Wyoming hideout known as Hole-in-the-Wall.

By 1900 the Wild West was coming to an end. Law and order were closing in on gunmen like Butch. South America began to look like a safe haven for outlaws. Butch, the Sundance Kid, and Etta Place (Sundance's girlfriend) bought a ranch in Argentina. From 1902 to 1906 they worked the ranch and stayed out of trouble.

Their attempts to go straight ended in 1906. With the law closing in, the three friends turned again to crime. In the months that followed they robbed banks and mines in Argentina and Bolivia. Then Etta fell ill and returned to the United States.

Chapman reported that Butch and Sundance ran out of luck in 1909. A troop of Bolivian soldiers caught up with *Los Bandidos Yanquis* (the Yankee bandits). The troop's captain drew his pistol and entered the house where the outlaws were eating. "Surrender, *señores*," he cried. Instead of raising his hands, Butch reached for his gun. His quick shot killed the captain.

The soldiers stationed outside opened fire. Rifle bullets peppered the house's adobe walls. The outlaws, armed only with pistols, were outgunned. Sundance told Butch, "Keep me covered. I'll get our rifles." A moment later he was sprinting across the courtyard, firing as he ran. A bullet spun him around and he fell, badly wounded.

Butch risked his own life to drag his friend back to the house. By then he was bleeding from several wounds. His cartridge belt was almost empty. Each time he tried to reach the rifles, the soldiers drove him back. At last darkness fell.

At about ten o'clock, the soldiers heard two shots. Then there was nothing but silence. Was it a trick? The long night crept past. At midday the soldiers rushed the house, but found only two bodies. As Chapman tells it, Butch had ended his friend's suffering with one shot. Then he used his last bullet on himself.[3]

At last, it seemed, the mystery of Butch's disappearance had been solved. His death in a bloody shootout satisfied the public's sense of right and wrong. Butch had lived by the gun and then died by the gun.

Butch Cassidy, however, refused to stay buried. There were those who questioned Chapman's facts. Old friends and family members claimed they had talked to the "dead" man. Butch had outfoxed the soldiers, they said. After returning home, he had taken a new name and built a new life.

In 1969 Hollywood revived the debate. In the hit film *Butch Cassidy and the Sundance Kid,* Paul Newman played Butch. Robert Redford appeared as Sundance. The film ignored the reports that Butch had survived the shootout in Bolivia. It ended with Butch and Sundance dashing into a hail of rifle bullets.

Did Hollywood choose the wrong ending for its film? Read this story of the famous outlaw. Then make up your own mind.

# 2

# A MAVERICK GROWS UP

The year 1866 holds a special place in the story of the Wild West. In February, Jesse James robbed his first bank. On April 13, the baby who grew up to be Butch Cassidy was born in Beaver, Utah. Max (short for Maximillian) and Annie Gillies Parker named their firstborn Robert LeRoy Parker. They called him LeRoy, but most people knew him as Bob.

As a boy, Max Parker had sailed west from England with his Mormon family. Iowa City was then the trailhead for the trek across the Great Plains. Faced with a shortage of wagons, the settlers loaded their goods onto two-wheeled handcarts. Then they pushed and pulled the carts 1,300 footsore miles to Utah.

Max's father helped build a woolen mill in Beaver. A few years later the church moved the older Parker farther south. Max stayed in Beaver to marry Annie Gillies.

The young husband found work carrying mail. Annie kept house and raised the children. Bob grew up to be a sturdy, happy child. His twelve younger brothers and sisters looked at him as their hero. To his mother's dismay, the fun-loving youngster resisted both schooling and religion.[1]

In 1879 the Parkers bought a Circle Valley homestead. That winter the bitter cold killed most of their cattle. Thirteen-year-old Bob took a job on the nearby Marshall ranch. His pay helped feed and clothe the family. The ranch became Bob's school. He learned about horses, cattle, and good times from the cowboys.

Max filed for a new homestead, but a second settler

*The Mormons of the mid-1800s dreamed of a new life in the West. To reach their promised land, they pushed and pulled their handcarts across 1,300 miles of wilderness. Butch Cassidy's parents and grandparents were among the hardy pioneers who made the long trek.*

claimed the same land. The local Mormon bishop who heard the case denied Max's claim. Bob was outraged. The bishop, he thought, was punishing his father for not being a good Mormon. Bob knew that Max sometimes skipped Sunday church meetings. He also liked to smoke now and then.[2] Never much of a churchgoer himself, the land dispute further battered Bob's faith.

The boy soon had his first brush with the law. One day he made the long ride into Circleville, only to find the general store closed. Instead of turning back, he broke into the store. Once inside, he picked out a pair of jeans. As promise of payment, he dropped an IOU on the counter. The break-in angered the shopkeeper, who swore out a complaint. The matter was settled out of court, but Bob's dislike of the law grew more intense.

At eighteen, Bob Parker stood 5 feet 9 inches and weighed 155 pounds. He had a quick, warm smile and a good sense of humor.[3] His best friend was a skilled horse and cattle thief named Mike Cassidy. Mike put Bob through a crash course in riding, shooting, and rustling. Pleased by the teenager's progress, he gave his prize pupil a pistol and saddle. Annie Parker saw the danger and tried to pry her son away from Mike. She failed. Later, when he needed an alias, Bob "borrowed" Mike's last name.

In the 1880s, vast herds of cattle that belonged to rich ranchers roamed the region. For much of the year no one tended the half-wild herds. Struggling ranchers

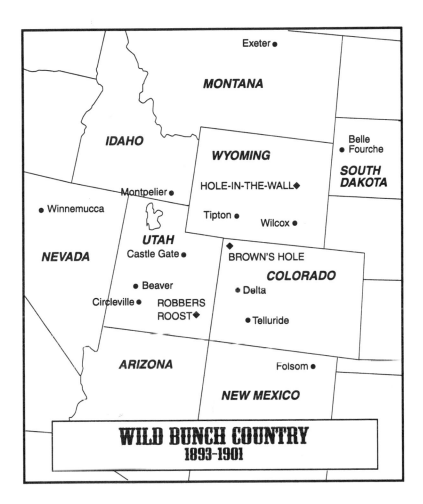

Exeter •

MONTANA

IDAHO

Belle
• Fourche

WYOMING

SOUTH
DAKOTA

HOLE-IN-THE-WALL◆

Montpelier •

• Winnemucca

Tipton •                    Wilcox •

◆

UTAH
Castle Gate •        BROWN'S HOLE

NEVADA

COLORADO

• Beaver            • Delta

Circleville •    ROBBERS
ROOST◆

• Telluride

ARIZONA              Folsom •

NEW MEXICO

**WILD BUNCH COUNTRY**
**1893-1901**

*Robert LeRoy Parker grew up around Circleville, Utah. When he took the outlaw trail, he changed his name to Butch Cassidy. This map shows some of the key sites in his story. Although his Wild Bunch gang roamed far and wide to commit robberies, they usually returned to hideouts in Robbers Roost, Brown's Hole, and Hole-in-the-Wall.*

sometimes rounded up the young unbranded cows. To prove ownership they marked these mavericks with their own brands.

In the spring of 1884 Bob went "mavericking" with some local ranchers. After crossing the nearby mountains the men collected a good-sized herd. Back on the Marshall ranch they branded their new livestock.

By June some of the cattle had drifted back to their home range. Angry cattlemen took one look at the fresh brands and filed charges. The older ranchers talked young Bob into taking the blame. Over his mother's protests, he signed a paper saying he had sold them the cattle. Then he saddled a fast horse and galloped out of town.[4] Ahead lay Utah's badlands and Robbers Roost.

*Butch began his outlaw life by rounding up mavericks. With large herds roaming free on the range, it was easy to find young, unbranded cows. Back at their home spread, Butch and his rancher friends put their own brands on the cattle.*

# 3

# A BANK JOB AND A NEW NAME

For the next few years Bob dropped out of sight. That was easy to do in the lonely Robbers Roost country of southeast Utah. He rode trails that appeared on no maps. Thanks to his skill with horses, he could always find work as a cowboy. When honest work grew tiresome, he stole horses and sold them. He still had a conscience, however. To protect his father's good name, he called himself George Cassidy. In good times he sent money home to his family.

Always restless, Bob moved on to southwest Colorado. Near the mining town of Telluride, he found work as a mule skinner. His team hauled silver ore down to the mills in the San Miguel Valley. Tiring of the hard work, Bob quit and returned to Robbers Roost. There he hooked up with a gang led by Bill and Tom McCarty. As a member of the McCarty gang, Bob became a regular on the owlhoot trail. Until this time he had only flirted with the outlaw life.

In the spring of 1889 the gang was short of cash. Bob told his new friends about the mine payrolls kept in Telluride's bank. With Tom McCarty and Matt Warner beside him, he returned to Telluride. By day the three men studied the San Miguel Valley Bank.[1] At night they drank and gambled in the town's saloons.

On the morning of June 24, the outlaws struck. When they saw the cashier leave the bank, they moved in. Tom

*At age 17, Butch posed with his horse for this portrait. Soon after this photo was taken he changed his name to Cassidy. That change marked the true start of the career that made him one of the Wild West's most famous outlaws.*

*When he tired of herding cattle, Butch found work as a mule skinner in Colorado. Hauling silver ore from Telluride to the mills in the valley below was hard work. Butch soon turned his thoughts to more profitable employment, such as stealing the mine's payroll.*

held the horses and Bob guarded the door. Matt, dressed in a fine town suit, walked into the bank. He handed the teller a fake check, then pointed a gun at him. "Come on in, boys," he called. "It's all right."[2]

Bob ran in, buckskin bags ready. He grabbed the money from the cash drawer and made a quick trip to the vault. When he left, the bags were bulging with $20,550. In 1889 this was a small fortune.

The robbers ran to their horses and galloped out of town. On Keystone Hill, Bert Charter was waiting with fresh mounts. Back in Telluride, Sheriff J. A. Beattie quickly called out a posse. One brave rider had already taken up the chase. He caught up with the fleeing outlaws as they were changing horses. No fool, he stopped at the foot of Keystone Hill.

The posse soon caught up with the advance scout. The man pointed at the bank robbers, who were still changing saddles. Bert saw the danger and took quick action. First he tied a small fallen tree to the tail of one of the horses. Then he shooed the horse toward the

*Butch joined Tom McCarty's gang in the spring of 1889. One of his first targets was the San Miguel Valley Bank in Telluride (steepled building, center left). The gang rode away from the raid with $20,550 in Butch's buckskin bags.*

posse. The tree scraped and bounced as the frightened horse bolted down the trail. The noise panicked the posse's horses. By the time the lawmen regained control, the gang was gone.

As soon as they felt safe the gang shared the loot. Then they went on a wild spree in the towns near their hideout. Bob liked whiskey, but the McCarty boys drank too much to suit him. He soon left the gang, drifting from job to job.

One account says he picked up his nickname during this time. Drawn north to Wyoming, he found work in a Rock Springs meat market. The townsfolk liked the friendly young butcher. He gave honest service and kept candy in his pockets for their children. It seemed natural to call him "Butch," a nickname often given to butchers.[3]

Butch was too footloose to stay tied to a town job. After leaving Rock Springs he punched cows in the Brown's Hole region of northeast Utah. When spring came, Butch teamed up with Al Hainer. The partners bought a ranch on Horse Creek near Lander, Wyoming. The local paper noted that the men planned to raise fine horses. In town, their free-spending ways made friends quickly. The locals did not guess that Butch was living high on stolen money.

# 4

# BUTCH'S LUCK TURNS SOUR

Butch and Al did not last long as horse breeders. They spent too much time in saloons and at Robbers Roost. Within the year they sold the ranch and roamed more widely. Even so, they always had money in their jeans. This alerted the local cattle barons, since someone was stealing their horses and cattle. They kept a close watch on Butch and Al.

One August day in 1891 Billy Nutcher appeared on the scene. Butch liked the looks of the three horses Billy was leading. The man was a known horse thief, but he swore these horses were his. Butch bought the story— and the horses. The matter might have ended there, but for rancher Otto Franc.

On August 28, Franc swore out a complaint. Butch and Al, he claimed, were riding stolen horses. Staying one jump ahead of the law, Butch and Al hid near

Auburn, Wyoming. At last, in April 1892, Deputy Sheriff Bob Calverly caught up with them.

Calverly and a second lawman found Butch dozing on a cot. Calverly later wrote, "I told [Butch] I had a warrant for him and he said: 'Well, get to shooting,' and with that we both pulled our guns."[1] In the struggle that followed, Butch's shot went wild. Calverly's first three shots missed, too. A fourth bullet creased Butch's scalp, stunning him. Al gave up without a fight. The deputy handcuffed his prisoners and took them to jail.

On July 30, the partners were freed on $400 bail. Trial was delayed another ten months so that two key witnesses could testify. On June 20, 1893, in a district court at Lander, Butch's lawyer asked for a further delay. This time it was two of Butch's witnesses who could not be found. The judge refused the request. Despite that setback the trial went well for the defense. The men on the jury liked Butch. They found him not guilty.

Butch's ordeal was not over. Otto Franc had filed a second complaint on June 19. This time he charged Butch with stealing the second of the three Nutcher horses. After making bail, Butch and Al parted ways. Friends had convinced Butch that his partner was working for Franc.

The second case came to trial in July 1894. A new jury convicted Butch of horse stealing, but set Al free. Looking back it seems clear that Butch knew he was buying stolen stock. He did not feel guilty. Franc, he believed,

*Butch posed for his prison mug shot at Laramie, Wyoming, in 1894. Although he showed little repentance in this photo, he turned out to be a model prisoner. After serving 18 months of a two-year sentence, he was given a pardon. Legend says he won his release by promising to leave Wyoming alone in the future.*

had set up the sale to trap him.[2] On July 10, the judge sentenced Butch to two years of hard labor. In those days that was a light sentence. Many horse thieves ended up on the end of a rope. Some oldtimers say that Butch left a sweetheart behind when he left for prison. If so, she may have been Mary Boyd, the pretty daughter of a pioneer settler. In later years, Mary claimed she had lived with Butch as his "common laws wife."[3]

Butch, who hated being locked up, learned to cope with prison life. He exercised in the prison yard and made new friends. With his pocket money he bought books, candy, and tobacco.

In all, Butch served eighteen months in the Laramie prison. Legend has it that he won early release by making a pledge to the governor. "If you will pardon me," Butch said, "I will promise to leave the state of Wyoming alone." Trusting Butch to keep his word, Governor Richards signed the papers.[4]

On January 19, 1896, Butch left prison a free man. He was also a harder and more bitter man. Prison, he claimed later, had truly turned him into an outlaw.[5]

Clerks kept track of Butch's stay at Laramie on a single page of the prison record book. The personal data is correct, except for showing his age as 32. Butch was only 28 when he entered prison.

# 5

# THE WILD BUNCH

---

Fresh from prison, Butch looked for work as a cowhand. No one would hire him. His past hung over him like a dark cloud.

Butch shrugged and returned to the owlhoot trail. This time he planned to go for the big money—banks, trains, and payrolls. That meant he would need a tough gang beside him. To insure the gang's safety, he would also need secure hiding places.

Butch carried a map of good hideouts in his head. For his northern headquarters he chose Hole-in-the-Wall in central Wyoming. The Red Wall, a steep cliff fifty miles in length, sheltered this lush valley. The single game trail into the valley could be hidden by a boulder.

Brown's Hole, near the Colorado-Wyoming border, served as a second hideout. Butch and Elzy Lay built a cabin there. They picked a high rocky site now known as Cassidy's Point. Choosing a third safe haven was easy. Ever since his youth, Butch had ridden the Robbers Roost country of southeast Utah.

By ones and twos, a band of gunmen answered Butch's call. The gang, he told them, would be called "the Train Robbers Syndicate."[1] The newspapers of the day invented a more colorful name. Headline writers made the gang famous as "The Wild Bunch."

Butch's best friend in the Wild Bunch was William Ellsworth "Elzy" Lay. Elzy was an expert horseman and

*Western outlaws could hide out for months in the rugged canyons of Robbers Roost. Butch knew this country well, and used it to his advantage. It is easy to imagine that the Wild Bunch once laughed at their pursuers from this viewpoint at Dead Horse Point.*

*Harvey Logan, better known as Kid Curry, was Butch's chief lieutenant. If there was gunplay during a robbery, Logan was likely to be involved. Butch respected his courage, but thought he was too ready to shoot people.*

gunman. Unlike Butch, who never married, Elzy and his wife raised two daughters. Butch called him "the educated member" of the group.[2] He counted on Elzy to plan the gang's train and bank robberies.

Harry Longabaugh was a second mainstay of the Wild Bunch. At seventeen, Harry had spent time in the Sundance, Wyoming, jail. Afterward everyone called him the Sundance Kid. He was slow to smile, dressed like a dandy, and liked his liquor. His foes knew he was a crack shot. Butch thought Sundance was too quick on the trigger.

The Wild Bunch attracted more than its share of top guns. Harvey Logan, better known as Kid Curry, was short, dark, and deadly. The quick-tempered Kid was second-in-command. Butch praised him as "the bravest man I ever knew."[3] Henry "Bob" Meek shared Butch's Mormon background. The two men had met while working as mule skinners. Ben Kilpatrick, a six-footer and a quick-draw expert, was called "the Tall Texan." Despite a disfigured left eye, he was popular with the ladies. Quiet Bill Carver also came from Texas. The gang never let him forget the day he fought a losing battle with a skunk.

That summer the gang heard that Matt Warner was in jail. To raise cash to pay for his friend's lawyer, Butch decided to rob a bank. The bank in Montpelier, Idaho, looked like a good bet. The town's location, he saw, offered an easy escape route into Wyoming. Butch worked on a nearby ranch while he scouted the bank.[4]

On August 13, 1896, three men hit the bank at closing time. Meek held the horses while Butch and Elzy slipped inside. Elzy held the bank clerks at gunpoint while Butch scooped up the money. Moments later they walked out with $6,615 in greenbacks and $1,000 in gold. As the outlaws raced out of town, a posse saddled up and rode in pursuit. That was when careful planning paid off. A fourth gang member was waiting with fresh mounts at Montpelier Pass. With their horses tiring, the posse gave up the chase.

Matt's well-paid lawyer lost the case. After the trial Butch offered to break his friend out of jail. Matt refused. He did not want to risk being shot in a jailbreak.

# 6

# A SNOWFALL OF GREENBACKS

---

The Wild Bunch pulled only a few jobs a year. The months between holdups gave the gang time to relax. Also, Butch needed time to plan each robbery. In the spring of 1897, he decided to specialize in trains and payrolls.

On April 21, the Denver & Rio Grande chugged into Castle Gate, Utah. Paymaster E. L. Carpenter was on hand to pick up the Pleasant Valley Coal Company payroll. Butch and Elzy Lay had waited a week for this moment. As Carpenter and his aides walked past, Butch stepped forward. He jammed his pistol into the paymaster's ribs and grabbed the payroll satchel. Elzy took a smaller bag from one of the aides. Moments later the outlaws were raising dust as they galloped out of town.

Carpenter gathered a small posse and ran to the waiting train. Uncoupled from its cars, the engine was soon whizzing down Pine Canyon gorge. No one saw Butch and Elzy, hidden behind a shed while they changed horses. From there the outlaws turned south, leaving two posses fanning out to the north. Three changes of horses later, the two men circled back toward Brown's Hole.[1]

The gang soon spent most of the $8,800 payroll on good times. Townsfolk welcomed the Wild Bunch at times like these. No one complained if Butch and the boys shot up the place. They paid saloonkeepers a dollar for every bullet hole they left in a bar.[2]

Less than two months later the Wild Bunch hit another bank. This time the target was Belle Fourche, South Dakota. Some accounts say that Butch rode with

*This express car shows the effects of two dynamite blasts set by the Wild Bunch. The first charge blew the door off. The second tore the safe apart—and sent wads of paper money soaring skyward. Here, sightseers from Wilcox, Wyoming, check out the wreckage.*

*Dynamite also played a key role in the Tipton, Wyoming, robbery. Three charges of dynamite blew the safe and wrecked the express car. Butch claimed that the gang rode off with $45,000 that day.*

the gang that day. Others insist that Kid Curry was in charge. Only one fact is certain. The Wild Bunch could not have pulled off all the jobs charged to their account.

After Belle Fourche, the gang took a two-year break. The men had plenty of cash and the law was closing in. In 1898 some of them joined the Army and fought in the Spanish-American War. Butch and Elzy hired on at the WS Ranch in Alma, New Mexico. Butch introduced himself as Jim Lowe. The manager liked the way he handled cattle and made him foreman. Teamed with Elzy, Butch kept the ranch running smoothly.[3]

The holiday from crime ended in June 1899. The war was over, and the gang was coming together again. Butch set his sights on a new target.

At 2:18 A.M. on June 2, the Overland Flyer was

heading toward Wilcox, Wyoming. Engineer W. R. Jones braked the train when he saw a red lantern ahead. As the engine slid to a stop, two masked men stepped out of the darkness. They forced the crew to uncouple the express car and engine. Then they ordered Jones to pull the express car across a nearby bridge. When the engineer was slow to obey, Kid Curry pistol-whipped him.

Four more masked men ran up and hammered on the express car. The frightened clerk refused to open the door. The outlaws solved the problem by blowing the door off with dynamite. After the smoke cleared they rolled the unconscious clerk out of the car. Then they dynamited the safe. The blast blew wads of paper money skyward. Soon it seemed to be snowing green- backs. Sticky reddish drops stained some of the bills. The "blood" turned out to be juice from a crate of raspberries.[4] As the dust settled, the outlaws took over $30,000 from the shattered safe.

Heavy rain bogged down the gang's getaway. Even though the outlaws changed horses three times, a posse tracked and cornered them. In the shootout that fol- lowed, Kid Curry killed Sheriff Joe Hazen. With their leader dead, the other lawmen broke off the chase.

Was Butch one of the masked men? If so, he broke the hands-off-Wyoming pledge he had made three years before. Even if he were not there, he most likely planned the job. Either way, his picture went up on wanted posters throughout the region.

# 7

# ONE STEP AHEAD OF THE LAW

---

The Wild Bunch struck again on July 11, 1899. Butch may have planned the job, but Elzy and Kid Curry carried it out. The outlaws stopped a train near Folsom, New Mexico, and made off with $30,000. A posse surprised the fleeing gang members at Turkey Creek. Three lawmen were killed in the firefight that followed. Though badly wounded, Elzy escaped. But he was captured that fall and sent to prison.

Law and order were becoming the new spirit of the West. The Union Pacific hired the Pinkerton National Detective Agency to catch the Wilcox train robbers. One by one, lawmen and detectives found the gang's hideouts. Posses made use of the railroads, the telephone, and the telegraph to cut off escape routes. Fast horses no longer guaranteed safety.

Butch spent the winter of 1899 in Texas. Perhaps he

was tiring of being hunted. He hired a Salt Lake lawyer to ask for amnesty. The governor of Utah said no, but the lawyer had better luck with the railroad. Drop all charges, he said, and Butch will go straight. A meeting was arranged, but a storm delayed the railroad officials. When they failed to appear, Butch was certain he had been double-crossed.[1]

On August 29, 1900, the Wild Bunch stopped a Union Pacific train outside Tipton, Wyoming. Butch was not there, but Kid Curry was. Because the train was stopped on an incline, Curry allowed the crew to set the brakes

*The railroads hired a superposse to hunt down the Wild Bunch. Some of the toughest lawmen in the West rode a fast train that was ready to go at a moment's notice. Here, six members of the superposse pose outside their Union Pacific stable car.*

on the passenger cars. Then he ordered the engineer to pull the express and mail cars to a safe distance. After blowing the safe with three charges of dynamite, the outlaws vanished. The railroad announced that the raid had netted only $50.40. Butch laughed at that statement. The gang had ridden off with a cool $45,000, he later wrote. The express car clerk backed his claim.[2]

The railroads fought back by offering rewards. They also put some of the West's best marksmen and trackers on a special train. Each man carried field glasses and a high-powered rifle. The train was equipped with a loading ramp, horse stalls, and a fast engine. It stood on a Wyoming siding, ready to go.[3]

Butch did not want to tangle with the superposse. For his next target he chose a town far to the west. On September 19, Butch, Sundance, and Bill Carver hit the bank at Winnemucca, Nevada. The bank president took one look at their pistols and opened the vault. The outlaws stuffed $32,640 into sacks and herded five hostages out the back door. Then they mounted their horses and rode out of town, guns blazing. Carver almost spoiled the getaway. He dropped a bag of gold coins and foolishly stopped to retrieve it.

A telephone call sent lawmen from the next town in hot pursuit. The chase lasted for days, but the gang owned faster horses. After the posse turned back, the outlaws headed to Fort Worth, Texas. The five men felt safe there and had a good time spending the bank's

*The Wild West that Butch Cassidy grew up in was changing fast. Outlaws had once been able to outride news of their robberies. Now, the telegraph spread the news at lightning speed. In this engraving, a Pony Express rider passes a crew putting up the wires that put him out of work, too.*

money. They bought stylish suits and even posed for a group photo. As a joke, Butch sent a copy to Winnemucca. His note thanked the bank for its donation.[4]

On July 3, 1901, the Great Northern Coast Flyer stopped for water near Wagner, Montana. Kid Curry jumped aboard. After crawling over the coal tender, he took command of the engine. A volley of warning shots sent passengers ducking back into the cars. Once again, the express car was uncoupled and pulled up the track. Once again, a dynamite blast cracked the safe. The outlaws were $65,000 richer when they rode away.

Butch knew it was time to break up the Wild Bunch. After outriding the pursuit, the men shook hands. Then, two by two, they rode off to start new lives.[5]

# 8

# LOS BANDIDOS YANQUIS

---

Butch had been told that Argentina did not extradite American outlaws. That vast country, with its growing cattle industry, looked like a perfect refuge. Sundance agreed to go with him. Their long trip began with a stop in New York City. Like any tourists they spent their days enjoying the sights of the big city.

Sundance took Etta Place with him. Some sources say Etta was a Denver schoolteacher. Others say she met Sundance while working in a Texas "sporting house." In *The Outlaw Trail,* Robert Redford calls her the granddaughter of an English lord.[1] Whatever her background, she was not a burden. Brave, green-eyed, and a crack shot, Etta rode as well as most men.

In February 1902, Sundance and Etta sailed for Argentina. To confuse the Pinkertons, Butch left by way of Canada. From there he caught a ship bound for England.

At Liverpool he boarded a cattle boat headed for South America.

In April 1902, the three fugitives met in Buenos Aires. They put $12,000 in a new bank account and bought land in southern Argentina. The remote ranch at Chubut was soon stocked with sheep, cattle, and horses. Butch and Sundance enjoyed their new roles as gentlemen ranchers. Etta served as hostess and helped work the ranch. She often put on riding pants and rode bareback at a gallop.

For four years the trio lived a peaceful life. Butch even urged friends back home to join him. In the eyes of the law, however, he was still a wanted man. In 1906 an American cattle buyer recognized the fugitives. Eager to collect a reward, the man asked the local police to

*Harry Longabaugh (the Sundance Kid) and Etta Place posed for this portrait while visiting New York City in 1902. Dressed in the height of fashion, the pair looked ready to enter high society. They left soon afterward to take up a new life as cattle ranchers in Argentina.*

make an arrest.[2] Luckily, the law moved slowly in that part of the world. Butch and Sundance had time to sell the ranch before they moved northward.

Butch had guessed wrong about finding refuge in Argentina. He guessed right when he said that South America was ripe for plucking. Over the next year he and Sundance started a minor crime wave. With Etta holding the horses, they robbed four banks, two express trains, and four pack trains.[3] Etta rode side-by-side with the men until illness forced her to return to the United States. Her outlaw days were over.

The region buzzed with stories of *Los Bandidos Yanquis*. A few of the jobs produced big payoffs. In Rio Galleos a bank vault yielded $20,000. The outlaws often hid in Indian villages. Gifts of gold and candy bought food, lodging, and safety. The Indians kept a stony silence when questioned by the police.[4]

The partners found honest work between holdups. In the spring of 1907 Butch took a job at the Concordia Tin Mines in Bolivia. He called himself Jim Maxwell. A week later the mine hired Sundance, who signed on as Enrique Brown. From time to time "Jim" and "Enrique" rode off to hijack mine payrolls. In 1908 manager Clement Glass learned their real names. Holding them at gunpoint, he warned them not to rob his mine. Butch and Sundance did not argue. They never stole from their friends.

Mine official Percy Seibert became one of those friends. He and his wife shared Sunday meals with the

*The Wild Bunch did not believe in saving for a rainy day. After robbing the bank in Winnemucca, Nevada, they headed for Fort Worth, Texas. There, during a wild spending spree, they posed for this famous portrait. Seated, from the left: Sundance, Ben Kilpatrick, and Butch. Standing: Bill Carver and Harvey Logan.*

outlaws. One night in 1909, Butch said, "I guess it's time to pull out."[5] Seibert thought his friend was looking older than his years. Soon afterward, *Los Bandidos* held up another mule train. As part of his loot, Butch helped himself to a fine silver-gray mule. Days later, at San Vicente, a constable spotted the mule. Knowing he was outgunned, he called in a troop of cavalry.

The gunfight that ends the film *Butch Cassidy and the Sundance Kid* followed. The soldiers seemed certain that the dead men were Butch and Sundance. Seibert, who knew the men well, confirmed the deaths.

The news slowly made its way northward. The leaders of the Wild Bunch, it seemed, had died with their boots on.

# 9

# DEAD OR ALIVE?

The dead do not come back to life. But many people swear Butch Cassidy did return from Bolivia. This "new" Butch, they tell us, called himself William T. Phillips. As Phillips, he married, built a business, and raised a child.

Let's look at the facts we do have. Lula Parker Betenson tells her version in *Butch Cassidy, My Brother.* Arthur Chapman's story of his death was more fiction than fact, she insisted. Lula goes into great detail in describing a 1925 visit with her brother.

How does the "Butch-didn't-die" crowd explain Percy Seibert's role? They insist that Seibert lied to Arthur Chapman. He may have wanted the world to *think* his friend was dead. Given a fresh start, Butch would be free to build a new life. Researchers have found that the Bolivian army has no record of the San

Vicente gunfight. Western author Larry Pointer did his best to find the truth. His research convinced him that William Phillips really was Butch Cassidy.

According to Pointer, Phillips first appeared in Adrian, Michigan, in the spring of 1908. That was the year *before* Butch's reported death. He told his neighbors that he owned a machine shop in Iowa. Within a few weeks he met, courted, and married Gertrude Livesay.

The couple soon headed south to Arizona. The desert climate, they hoped, would help Gertrude's asthma. Phillips later claimed that he served as a sharpshooter for Pancho Villa during this time. The Mexican bandit chief paid him six dollars a day, he said. Two years later, the couple moved to Spokane, Washington. En route they visited Hole-in-the-Wall.

In Spokane, Phillips worked as a draftsman. He also went prospecting for gold in Alaska. There he met the great lawman Wyatt Earp. Earp was certain the man called Phillips was really Butch Cassidy.[1] Back in Spokane, Phillips invented an adding machine and started the Phillips Manufacturing Company. In 1919 William and Gertrude adopted a baby boy. In 1925 the family moved to a fine large home. Times were good.

That same summer Phillips told his wife a lie. He said he was going to South America on business. The story freed him to travel back into his past. After looking up old friends in Wyoming, he drove to his family home in Utah. Forty-one years had passed since he left. Max

*Butch's family was convinced that the man known as William Phillips really was their son and brother. If their story is true, Butch returned from South America and started a new career as a machinist-inventor. He married, started a manufacturing company, and lived a largely blameless life.*

was eighty-one, but the old man was certain this man was his son.[2]

Phillips's business failed in 1930. From 1933 on he worked at odd jobs. In his spare time he wrote his version of Butch's life. He put his heart into *The Bandit Invincible*, but no one would publish the poorly-written story. At one low point in 1935 Phillips thought of returning to crime. His plot to kidnap a wealthy Spokane man never went past the planning stage.[3] By that time Phillips was an ailing sixty-nine. Riddled with cancer, he died at the county poor farm in 1937.

Could William Phillips have been Butch Cassidy? *The Bandit Invincible* contains details that only Butch could have known. A handwriting expert compared letters written by the two men. The expert felt certain the same hand produced both letters.[4] On the other hand, Phillips did appear in Michigan at least six months before the famous shootout in Bolivia.

Whatever the truth of Phillips's claims, Butch's legend lives on. The reasons are easy to understand. Most western outlaws were grim, deadly killers. Butch was a sunny, bighearted man. When he stole, he never robbed poor people. He also avoided gunplay whenever he could. And, his admirers say, he went out in a final blaze of rifle fire. That's the stuff of which legends are made.

*Paul Newman (left) played Butch and Robert Redford took the role of Sundance in Hollywood's* Butch Cassidy and the Sundance Kid. *In the film's final dramatic scene, the outlaws dash headlong into a volley of rifle fire.*

# NOTES BY CHAPTER

## Chapter 1

1. *Washington Post* (April 23, 1930).

2. Arthur Chapman, "Butch Cassidy," *Elks Magazine* (April 1930).

3. Ibid.

## Chapter 2

1. Lula Parker Betenson, *Butch Cassidy, My Brother* (Provo, Utah: Brigham Young University Press, 1975), p. 38.

2. Larry Pointer, *In Search of Butch Cassidy* (Norman, Okla.: University of Oklahoma Press, 1977), p. 44.

3. Charles Kelly, *The Outlaw Trail: A History of Butch Cassidy and His Wild Bunch* (New York: Bonanza Books, 1959), p. 10.

4. Betenson, pp. 44–48.

## Chapter 3

1. Some sources say there were four robbers that day in Telluride.

2. *Rocky Mountain News* (June 27, 1889).

3. Pearl Baker, *The Wild Bunch at Robbers Roost* (New York: Abelard-Schuman, 1971), p. 185.

## Chapter 4

1. Larry Pointer, *In Search of Butch Cassidy* (Norman, Okla.: University of Oklahoma Press, 1977), pp. 72–73.

2. Ibid., p. 76.

3. Ibid., pp. 58–59.

4. Alan Swallow, ed., *The Wild Bunch* (Denver: Sage Books, 1966), p. 38.

5. Lula Parker Betenson, *Butch Cassidy, My Brother* (Provo, Utah: Brigham Young University Press, 1975), p. 96.

## Chapter 5

1. Pearl Baker, *The Wild Bunch at Robbers Roost* (New York: Abelard-Schuman, 1971), p. 188.

2. James D. Horan and Paul Sann, *Pictorial History of the Wild West* (New York: Bonanza, 1954), p. 54.

3. Larry Pointer, *In Search of Butch Cassidy* (Norman, Okla.: University of Oklahoma Press, 1977), p. 100.

4. Charles Kelly, *The Outlaw Trail: A History of Butch Cassidy and His Wild Bunch* (New York: Bonanza Books, 1959), p. 95.

## Chapter 6

1. Lula Parker Betenson, *Butch Cassidy, My Brother* (Provo, Utah: Brigham Young University Press, 1975), pp. 123–125.

2. Charles Kelly, *The Outlaw Trail: A History of Butch Cassidy and His Wild Bunch* (New York: Bonanza Books, 1959), p. 160.

3. Ibid., pp. 249–250.

4. Betenson, p. 136.

## Chapter 7

1. Charles Kelly, *The Outlaw Trail: A History of Butch Cassidy and His Wild Bunch* (New York: Bonanza Books, 1959), pp. 266–271.

2. Larry Pointer, *In Search of Butch Cassidy* (Norman, Okla.: University of Oklahoma Press, 1977), p. 169.

3. James D. Horan and Paul Sann, *Pictorial History of the Wild West* (New York: Bonanza, 1954), p. 217.

4. Pearl Baker, *The Wild Bunch at Robbers Roost* (New York: Abelard-Schuman, 1971), p. 193.

5. Pointer, p. 183.

## Chapter 8

1. Robert Redford, *The Outlaw Trail* (New York: Grosset and Dunlap, 1978), p. 188.

2. *Clarin*, Buenos Aires, Argentina (May 2, 1970).

3. Larry Pointer, *In Search of Butch Cassidy* (Norman, Okla.: University of Oklahoma Press, 1977), p. 201.

4. James D. Horan and Paul Sann, *Pictorial History of the Wild West* (New York: Bonanza, 1954), p. 231.

5. Ibid., p. 237.

## Chapter 9

1. Larry Pointer, *In Search of Butch Cassidy* (Norman, Okla.: University of Oklahoma Press, 1977), p. 220.

2. Lula Parker Betenson, *Butch Cassidy, My Brother* (Provo, Utah: Brigham Young University Press, 1975), pp. 177–179.

3. Pointer, p. 246.

4. Ibid. p. 25.

# GLOSSARY

**adobe**—Sundried bricks made of clay and straw. A building made of these bricks is also called an adobe.

**alias**—An assumed name. Western outlaws often used aliases to conceal their true identities.

**amnesty**—A legal document that forgives suspected criminals for any offenses they may have committed.

**bail**—Money paid to a court to guarantee the return of a suspect for trial.

**cattle barons**—A reference to the owners of large cattle ranches in the Wild West. Because of their power and wealth, these owners sometimes ruled their lands like medieval lords.

**common-law wife**—In the Wild West, men and women sometimes set up housekeeping without going through a marriage ceremony. After the couple lived together as husband and wife for a time, the woman gained a legal status known as common-law wife.

**complaint**—A legal claim in which one citizen charges another with a financial or physical injury.

**constable**—A low-ranking lawman who keeps the peace in a town or village.

**dime novels**—Popular fiction printed in low-cost books and magazines during the late 1800s.

**express car**—A special baggage car equipped to carry a train's cargo of mail, gold, cash, and other valuables.

**extradite**—To return accused criminals to the state or country in which they will stand trial.

**greenbacks**—A slang term for United States paper money.

**gunslingers**—Outlaws and lawmen of the Wild West who settled arguments with their pistols.

**handcarts**—Small two-wheeled carts on which Mormon settlers carried their household goods across the Great Plains.

**IOU**—A promise to pay a debt. The initials stand for *I owe you*.

**jury**—A group of citizens sworn to judge the facts and give a verdict in a court case.

**legend**—A story that many people believe, but which is often untrue in whole or in part.

**mavericks**—In the Wild West, unbranded calves who were found roaming free. Tradition said that mavericks belonged to the first person to brand them.

**mule skinner**—Anyone who drove a mule team in the Wild West. The name was taken from the long leather whip the mule skinner used to control the team.

**owlhoot trail, riding the**—Wild West slang for choosing the life of an outlaw.

**pistol-whipped**—Beaten with a pistol.

**posse**—A group of citizens who join with lawmen to help capture fleeing outlaws.

**railroad tycoons**—A reference to the rich and powerful men who owned the railroads of the Wild West.

**rustler**—An outlaw who steals horses or cattle.

**"soiled dove"**—Wild West slang for a prostitute.

**Spanish-American War**—The 1898 war between Spain and the United States.

**sporting house**—Wild West slang for a house of prostitution.

**trailhead**—The city or town from which travelers set off on a wilderness trail.

# MORE GOOD READING ABOUT BUTCH CASSIDY

Baker, Pearl. *The Wild Bunch at Robbers Roost*. New York: Abelard-Schuman, 1971.

Betenson, Lula Parker (as told to Dora Flack). *Butch Cassidy, My Brother*. Provo, Utah: Brigham Young University Press, 1975.

Henry, Will. *Alias Butch Cassidy*. New York: Random House, 1967.

Horan, James D. *The Authentic Wild West: The Outlaws*. New York: Crown Publishers, 1977, pp. 227–290.

Horan, James D., and Paul Sann. *Pictorial History of the Wild West*. New York: Bonanza Books, 1954.

Kelly, Charles. *The Outlaw Trail: A History of Butch Cassidy and His Wild Bunch*. New York: Bonanza Books, 1959.

Pointer, Larry. *In Search of Butch Cassidy*. Norman, Okla.: University of Oklahoma Press, 1977.

Redford, Robert. *The Outlaw Trail*. New York: Grosset and Dunlap, 1978.

Swallow, Alan, ed. *The Wild Bunch*. Denver: Sage Books, 1966.

Trachtman, Paul, and editors of Time-Life Books. "Butch Cassidy's Wild Bunch: Last of the Old-Time Gangs," *The Gunfighters*. Alexandria, Va.: Time-Life Books, 1974.

# INDEX